The Really **Wild Life** of **Insects**™

PEANUT-HEAD BUGS

ANDREW HIPP

The Rosen Publishing Group's
PowerKids Press™
New York

For Dr. B. V. Ridout, whose thoughtful and readable work on Fulgora laternaria covered much ground that previously had been the domain of conjecture and anecdote

The author gratefully acknowledges Drs. P. J. DeVries and C. R. Bartlett for looking over an early draft of this manuscript.

Published in 2003 by The Rosen Publishing Group, Inc.
29 East 21st Street, New York, NY 10010

First Edition

Editor: Gillian Houghton
Book Design: Mike Donnellan, Michael de Guzman

Photo Credits: Cover, back cover, pp. 8, 11, 16, 19 © Robert & Linda Mitchell; p. 4 © James P. Rowan; p. 7 © M. Fogden/OSF/Animals Animals; p. 12 © Michael & Patricia Fogden/Corbis; p. 15 © Buddy Mays/Corbis; pp. 15 (inset), p. 20 © Doug Wechsler/Animals Animals.

Hipp, Andrew.
Peanut-head bugs / Andrew Hipp.
    p. cm. — (The really wild life of insects)
Summary: Introduces the insects of the Fulgoridae family, which live on the sap of Central and South American Simaruba trees and are sometimes called peanut-head bugs.
Includes bibliographical references (p.   ).
 ISBN 0-8239-6242-3 (lib. bdg.)
 1. Fulgoridae—Juvenile literature. [1. Fulgorids.] I. Title.
  QL527.F9 H56 2003
  595.7'52—dc21
                                                                2001006656

Manufactured in the United States of America

CONTENTS

A BUG WITH MANY NAMES

In the forests of Central America and northern South America lives a bug that goes by many names. Its head is long and round, like a peanut, so some people call it the peanut-head bug. People have claimed that the bug's head glows at night and have given the bug the name "lanternfly." The bug has been said to zigzag through the forests, killing everything it touches. For this reason, the bug is also called the snake-cicada and the flying snake. These stories are untrue. The peanut-head bug does not glow in the dark or harm animals. Instead it hides on rough tree bark, drinking sap and trying to avoid trouble.

The scientific name for the peanut-head bug is Fulgora, the name of the ancient Roman goddess of lightning.

THROAT-BEAKED BUGS

The peanut-head bug is closely related to the leafhopper, the spittlebug, and the cicada. Each of these insects has a strawlike mouth called a **proboscis**, or beak, attached to the base of the head. The proboscis appears to grow right out of the throat. For this reason, this group of bugs is called Auchenorrhyncha. The name Auchenorrhyncha comes from the Greek words meaning "throat" and "beak."

Bugs in the Auchenorrhyncha group, including the peanut-head bug, fold their outer pair of wings over their backs like a tent or a roof. The second pair of wings is folded underneath.

The bug's peanut-shaped "head" is actually an enlarged forehead. Its eyes are located above the base of its forelegs.

FUN FACTS
SCIENTISTS USUALLY RESERVE THE WORD "BUG" FOR INSECTS OF THE ORDER HEMIPTERA, WHICH INCLUDES THE AUCHENORRHYNCHA.

FUN FACTS
SIMARUBA TREES ARE FULL
OF POISONOUS CHEMICALS.
SCIENTISTS BELIEVE THAT
PEANUT-HEAD BUGS MUST
HAVE A WAY TO PROCESS
THESE CHEMICALS SAFELY.

PLANTSUCKERS AND PREY

A long, skinny tube called a labium forms the outer layer of a bug's proboscis. The labium is used to taste food and to feel the surface of plants and prey. Wrapped inside the labium are two long, razor-sharp organs called **stylets**. The stylets fit together like the closure of a zip-lock bag. Two canals run from the bases to the tips of the stylets. One canal carries a **saliva** that breaks down the bug's food. The other canal sucks up the juice. The peanut-head bug slides its stylets through the bark of Simaruba trees to reach the tasty sap inside. It squirts out a special kind of saliva that helps the stylets move easily inside the tree. The bug pierces plant **cells** inside the tree.

Peanut-head bugs enjoy the sugary water and fatty food stored inside plant cells.

WHAT'S IN THAT HEAD?

Inside the large "peanut" of a peanut-head bug is an extension of the bug's stomach. Scientists do not know for sure why the peanut-head bug has part of its stomach in its head, but they have some ideas. The large stomach and the blood vessels surrounding it might be a place to store energy from food. It might also help the bug escape from **predators**. The extended stomach lies right next to the flight muscles in the **thorax**. It might help to bring food energy to the flight muscles on a moment's notice. The muscles need this energy for the bug to fly to safety. Whatever its job, the extended stomach gives the peanut-head bug an unusual appearance.

The peanut-head bug's head is often filled with air bubbles. Without bubbles its fluid-filled head would be heavy in flight.

FUN FACTS
AT THE BEGINNING OF THE 1900S, SOME SCIENTISTS ARGUED THAT PEANUT-HEAD BUGS MIMICKED ALLIGATORS IN THEIR APPEARANCE.

LIZARD OR LUNCH?

The peanut-head bug has gray and white wings that closely match the bark of the Simaruba tree. It rests with its head pointing toward the sky and its wing tips pointing toward the ground. Its markings blend in with the upright pattern of the bark. The combination of behavior and coloration helps the peanut-head bug blend into its forest surroundings. The peanut-head bug may also mimic, or copy, lizards. The bug's large head looks like a lizard's head. The bug's body is about the same size as a lizard's body. Some scientists argue that these similarities fool some of the birds and lizards who might like to eat the peanut-head bug.

This peanut-head bug is well hidden by its coloring, but it is still at risk. Birds and lizards are fierce predators.

SURPRISE!

When a predator approaches a peanut-head bug, the bug might leap from its roost and give off a bad smell. If the predator catches the peanut-head bug by grabbing the peanut-shaped head in its beak or jaws, the bug has a back-up **defense**. Its wings open to reveal spots on its hind wings. These spots look like the eyes of a larger animal and often scare away a predator. Some scientists argue that the bug's head draws a predator's attention away from its wings. An attack on the bug's head leaves its wings unharmed. The bug can still surprise its attacker with its eyespots and fly away to safety.

A peanut-head bug spreads its wings to reveal large yellow eyespots (right and inset).

The egg of a peanut-head bug is about ⅕ inch (.5 cm) long, with a cap at one end. A newborn peanut-head bug **nymph** is about the same length as its egg. At birth the bug may have a shiny black body and a pale yellow head. It looks a bit like an adult bug, but the nymph has no wings. Its wings will develop as **wing pads** on the back of its thorax. Unlike an adult bug, it also has spines on the sides of its head. Like an adult bug, a peanut-head bug nymph has **antennae** that attach to its face just below the eyes. However, there are fewer **sensory organs** on the antennae of a nymph than on those of an adult bug.

This peanut-head bug, which lives in a Costa Rican rain forest, has the fully grown wings and antennae of an adult.

As do all insects, peanut-head bugs and their relatives lack skeletons inside their bodies. For this reason, insects are part of a group of animals called the **invertebrates**, which means "without backbones." Instead they have a hard shell called an **exoskeleton**. The exoskeleton provides protection and support for an invertebrate's muscles and organs. As an insect gets bigger, it must grow a larger exoskeleton and shed the old one. It does this several times. Each time it **molts**, a peanut-head bug goes through small changes. Its wing pads get a little larger. Its color changes slightly, and the spines on its legs grow larger and more numerous. The series of changes a bug undergoes as it grows and molts is called **incomplete metamorphosis**.

Fully grown peanut-head bugs are similar in size to some of the lizards that live in the trees with them.

MATING AND LAYING EGGS

After the fifth molt, a peanut-head bug nymph becomes an adult. When his wings are fully developed, the male begins to search for a mate. He watches for her and listens for sounds that she makes.

The female peanut-head bug spends her time eating in preparation for mating and laying about 100 eggs. After mating she lays her eggs in rows on tree trunks or branches. Most female throat-beaked bugs make tiny cuts in leaf tissue and lay their eggs in the plant. A female makes these cuts with the ovipositor, a tube-shaped organ on the tip of the female's **abdomen**.

These two peanut-head bugs live along the Amazon River, in Peru's Tambopata Candamo nature reserve.

PEANUT-HEAD MYTHS

In South America some people believe that peanut-head bugs deliver deadly stings to monkeys. In Brazil, newspapers have claimed that peanut-head bugs have destroyed herds of cattle. The bug's large size and funny shape often scare people, even though it is a harmless, plant-eating insect without a stinger.

Most of us will never see a peanut-head bug, but we can look for its relatives. We may find leafhoppers on the leaves or the branches of trees. We may hear cicadas singing outside in the summer. When we do, we can think of the peanut-head bug, an odd-looking insect with many names.

GLOSSARY

abdomen (AB-duh-min) The large, rear section of an insect's body.

antennae (an-TEH-nee) Thin, rodlike organs on the heads of insects, used in smelling and feeling.

cells (SELZ) Tiny, balloonlike or boxlike units that make up all living things.

defense (dih-FENS) A feature of a living thing that helps to protect it.

exoskeleton (ek-soh-SKEH-leh-tin) The hard, outer shell of an insect's body.

incomplete metamorphosis (in-kum-PLEET meh-tuh-MOR-fuh-sis) The series of changes that an insect undergoes when it changes from nymph to adult, resulting in an increase in size but not a great change in form.

invertebrates (in-VER-tih-brits) Animals that have an exoskeleton and no backbone.

molts (MOLTZ) Sheds skin, feathers, or an exoskeleton.

nymph (NIMF) A young insect in the process of incomplete metamorphosis. A nymph looks like a small adult but without fully grown wings.

predators (PREH-duh-terz) Animals that kill other animals for food.

proboscis (pruh-BAH-sis) Long, sucking mouthparts found on such insects as true bugs, leafhoppers and their relatives, bees, butterflies, and others.

saliva (suh-LY-vuh) Liquid in the mouth that breaks down food and helps it slide down the throat.

sensory organs (SENS-ree OR-gunz) Organs such as eyes or taste buds that provide the brain with information about the world.

stylets (STY-lets) Needle-shaped mouthparts made for cutting and for sucking juices.

thorax (THOR-aks) The middle segment of an insect's body, to which legs and wings attach.

wing pads (WING PADZ) Baby wings on the back of a nymph's thorax. Wings develop inside of wing pads only in insects that undergo incomplete metamorphosis.

INDEX

WEB SITES

To learn more about peanut-head bugs and their relatives, check out this Web site:
http://worldforest.geo.msu.edu/rfrc/tour/slide6.html

24